Corking

written by
Judy Ann Sadler

illustrated by Linda Hendry

KIDS CAN PRESS

To Laurie, Ricky and Valerie —
a corker of a publishing team!

First U.S. edition 1998

Kids Can Press acknowledges the financial support of the Government of Canada,
through the BPIDP, for our publishing activity.

Published in Canada by
Kids Can Press Ltd.
29 Birch Avenue
Toronto, ON M4V 1E2

Published in the U.S. by
Kids Can Press Ltd.
2250 Military Road
Tonawanda, NY 14150

www.kidscanpress.com

Edited by Laurie Wark
Designed by Karen Powers
Photographs by Steve Payne
Printed in Hong Kong, China, by Wing King Tong Company Limited

This book is limp sewn with a drawn-on cover.

CMC PA 95 0

Canadian Cataloguing in Publication Data

Sadler, Judy Ann, 1959–
    Corking

(Kids can do it)
ISBN 1-55074-265-5

1. Knitting — Juvenile literature. 2. Handicraft — Juvenile literature.
I. Hendry, Linda. II. Title. III. Series.

TT829.S34 1995   j746.43'2   C98-931446-4

Kids Can Press is a *Corus*™ Entertainment company

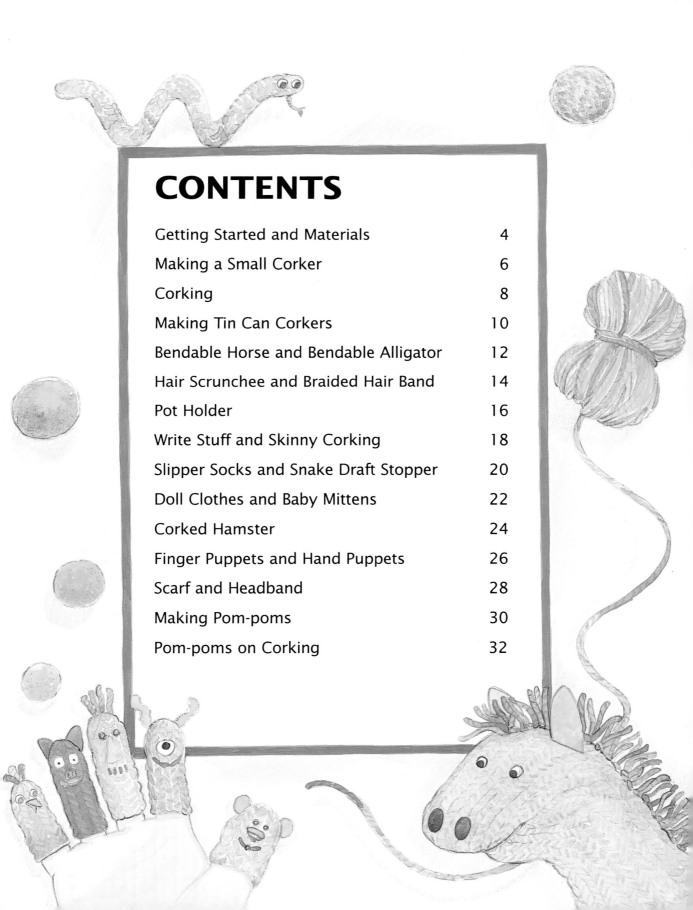

CONTENTS

GETTING STARTED

Would you believe that over the years a corker has been called a corking spool, spool loom, spool knitter, knitting spool, knitting knobby, knitting Nancy and even a Bizzy Lizzy? Nobody seems to know where all of these names came from, but corking has always been fun and easy no matter what you call it. By taking up corking you'll be carrying on an old, treasured craft.

With this book you will see how easy it is to make small corkers out of bathroom tissue rolls and large corkers out of big, empty tin cans. The corking you get from a small corker looks like a narrow, knitted tube. Use this corking to make bendable animals or coasters or to decorate your clothing. The corking you get from a tin can corker looks like round knitting. Use it to make a scarf, headband, slipper socks or a stuffed animal. You'll find all kinds of neat new projects and an easy way to make pom-poms to decorate your corking. Your corked crafts will make great gifts, too!

One of the best things about corking is that you can do it any time — while you're talking on the telephone, listening to music, riding in a car or spending time with your friends. And if you put it down, you can easily pick up and carry on from where you left off.

So, make a corker, grab some yarn and have a corking good time!

Materials

Yarn Yarn comes in many different colors, textures and types, such as wool, angora, mohair and cotton. For corking projects, you will find it easiest to use acrylic knitting worsted. It is a medium-thick yarn that is strong, inexpensive, washable and comes in an assortment of colors. Multi-colored yarn is especially fun to use for corking. Also, check to see if there is any leftover yarn around your home that you can use.

Corkers Save empty cardboard bathroom tissue rolls and tin cans in all sizes for making corkers. If you have a small store-bought corker, you can use it to make the small corked projects in this book.

Nails You will need smooth, thin finishing or common nails about 4 cm (1 1/2 inches) long to make corkers. These nails are available at hardware and building supply stores or you may have some around your home.

Tape Cloth tape, which is also called hockey or athletic tape, is great for making corkers because it is strong and comes in many colors. If you don't have cloth tape, you can use masking tape.

Yarn Needles You can use a tapestry, craft, plastic canvas or large blunt needle to finish off some of the projects. Make sure your needle has a rounded rather than sharp tip and a large eye (hole). You can use the needle to cork with, too, or use a plastic cocktail toothpick, opened bobby pin or very long, thin nail. Be sure to keep these things away from younger children.

Scissors Use scissors that have short blades and are sharp enough to cut yarn easily.

Other Stuff You may need a few other things for decorating your projects, such as pipe cleaners, moving eyes, polyester fiberfill, non-toxic white glue and felt or fabric scraps.

MAKING A SMALL CORKER

THINGS YOU NEED

bathroom tissue roll
scissors
cloth tape about 2.5 cm (1 inch) wide
8 smooth, thin nails about
  4 cm (1½ inches) long
felt or fabric scraps
white glue
rubber band

1 Make a lengthwise cut straight up the tube to open it.

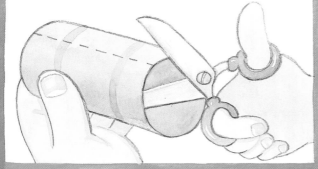

2 Cut six pieces of tape, each about 8 cm (3 inches) long.

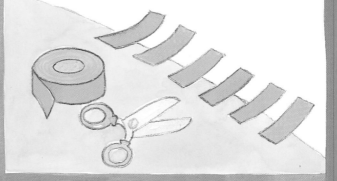

3 Roll the tube until it is doubled around. Attach the strips of tape down the entire length to hold this shape.

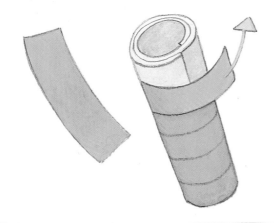

4 Cut another strip of tape 10 cm (4 inches) long and place it sticky side out along the top edge of the tube.

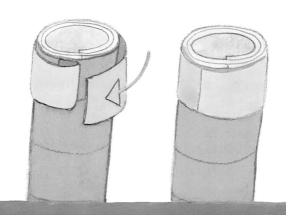

5 Hold two nails side by side and place them on the tape so that 1 cm (½ inch) of the nails is above the top of the tube.

6 Place a second pair of nails across from the first pair. Place two more pairs of nails across from each other so that you have four evenly spaced pairs of nails around the top of your tube.

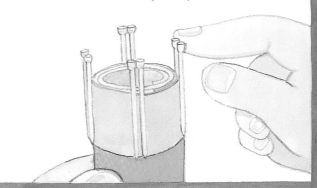

7 Use more tape to cover the nails and the sticky side of the tape along the top. Cut four narrow pieces of tape and place them in the spaces between the pairs of nails to help hold the nails in place.

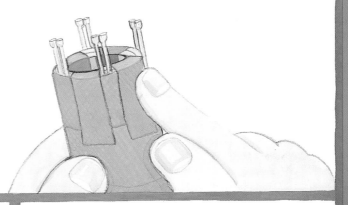

8 You can decorate your corker by wrapping colorful cloth tape around it or by gluing on a piece of felt or fabric.

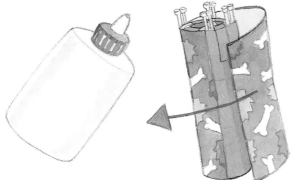

9 Place the rubber band around the middle of your corker as a handy spot to tuck your corking needle when you are not using it.

CORKING

THINGS YOU NEED

small corker

small ball of yarn

blunt yarn needle, bobby pin,
   plastic cocktail toothpick or
   a long, thin nail

scissors

1 Make a slip knot about 25 cm (10 inches) from the end of the yarn.

2 Place the slip knot loop over a pair of nails. Poke the yarn tail down the center of your corker.

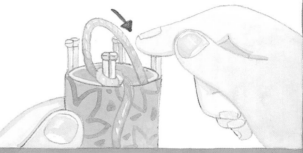

3 Bring the yarn from the ball behind the next pair of nails. Wind the yarn around this pair and bring it behind the next pair. Repeat this on the next two nail posts so that all the nails have yarn looped around them. You can hold the corker in your right or left hand and wind the yarn either way as long as you don't change directions in the middle of a project.

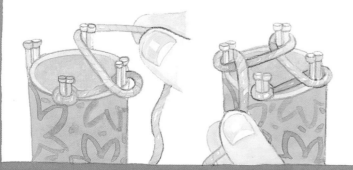

4 You should now have the yarn back to the nails with the slip knot on them. Wind the yarn in front of these nails, above the slip knot loop. Hold the yarn end in place with the fingers holding the corker.

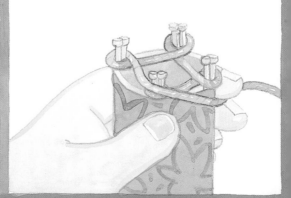

5 Poke the yarn needle down into the slip knot loop, being careful not to split the yarn. Pull the yarn loop toward you and lift it up and over the top line of yarn and the nails. Let it off your needle.

6 Turn the corker in your hand as you wind the yarn above the loops already on the nails. Continue to lift the bottom yarn over the top. Try to keep your stitches loose. Every once in a while pull down on the yarn tail hanging out the bottom.

7 To add a new color to your corking, cut off the yarn you are using, leaving a 5-cm (2-inch) tail. Knot the new color to the old one and keep corking. Tuck the knot into the center of the corking so that the ends do not show.

8 When you are measuring the length of your corking for a project, remember to include the part still inside your corker.

9 To finish off your corking, cut the yarn, leaving a 20-cm (8-inch) tail. Lift the loop off the set of nails you just corked and put it on the next set of nails. Do a regular corking stitch. Lift the leftover loop and put it on the next set of nails and so on until you are left with one loop on one set of nails.

10 Pull on the last loop to make it larger. Thread the yarn tail through it and pull it tight as you lift it off the nails.

MAKING TIN CAN CORKERS

THINGS YOU NEED

empty, clean tin can with the label removed

cloth tape

smooth, thin nails about 4 cm (1½ inches) long

felt or fabric scraps and white glue for decorating (optional)

1 Ask an adult to help you remove both ends of the tin can. If there are sharp pieces of tin sticking out, gently hammer them down and cover them with tape.

2 Tape over the top and bottom edges of your can.

3 Wrap two or three layers of tape around the top of the can, just under the rim, until the tape is even with the rim.

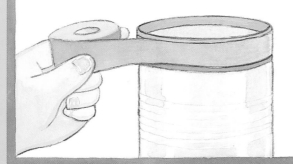

4 Place a strip of tape sticky side out along the top edge of the can. Place the nails around the top in the same way you did for the corker on page 7. There should be about 1.5 cm (⅝ inch) between each set of nails. Use the chart on page 11 to figure out how many nails you will need for each different-sized can corker.

CAN CORKER SIZES

Small can corker
156 mL (5 ½ fl oz)
18 nails (9 sets)

Medium can corker
398 mL (14 fl oz)
22 nails (11 sets) or
540 mL (19 fl oz)
26 nails (13 sets)

Large can corker
796 mL (28 fl oz)
34 nails (17 sets)

Huge can corker
1.1 kg or 2.84 L
(2 lb 7 oz or
100 fl oz)
40 nails (20 sets)

---

5 Cut more strips of tape to cover the sticky tape and nails. Try to press the tape snugly around the nails.

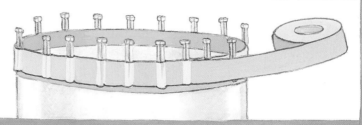

---

6 Place narrow pieces of tape in the spaces between each set of nails. Add a couple more rounds of tape to make sure the nails don't wiggle. You can decorate your can corker by gluing on felt or fabric or by wrapping colorful cloth tape around it.

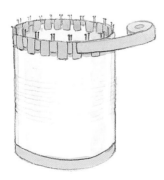

USING A TIN CAN CORKER

Get started on your tin can corker the same way as on a small corker (see page 8). Whenever you cork on a tin can corker, **it is important to loosen the loop that is left on the nails you just corked by pulling it forward.** If you don't do this, the yarn will be too tight to be lifted over the nails in the next round.

Instructions for taking your corking off the corker are included at the end of each tin can corking project.

BENDABLE HORSE

THINGS YOU NEED

3 pieces of small corking, two 20 cm
  (8 inches) long and one 15 cm (6 inches) long
3 pipe cleaners, each 30 cm (12 inches) long
scissors
yarn needle, yarn
safety pin
moving eyes or beads
white glue

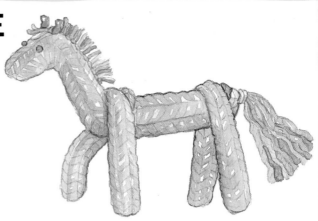

1 Hook the end of one of the pipe cleaners into the safety pin.

2 Poke the pin into the end of one of the corked pieces and weave it through to the other end. Trim off any extra pipe cleaner. (Usually the pipe cleaner will stay in place, but you can put a dab of glue on the ends to make sure it does.) Weave pipe cleaners into the other two corked pieces.

3 Shape the shorter bendable corked piece into a horse's head, neck and back. Wrap the other two pieces around the back to make legs.

4 Use a yarn needle to pull short pieces of yarn through the neck area to make a mane. Knot them in place. Make a long yarn tail — separate the strands of yarn to make the tail kinky. Glue on moving eyes or beads for the eyes. Poke a piece of pipe cleaner about 2.5 cm (1 inch) long through the corking above the eyes to make ears.

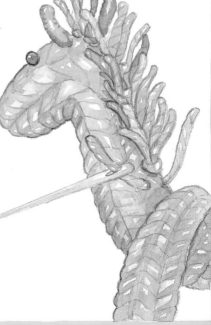

BENDABLE ALLIGATOR

THINGS YOU NEED

2 pieces of small corking, each 30 cm (12 inches) long

2 pieces of small corking, each 15 cm (6 inches) long

3 pipe cleaners, each 30 cm (12 inches) long

safety pin, yarn needle, yarn, white glue, scissors

moving eyes or 2 beads and 16 small white beads for teeth

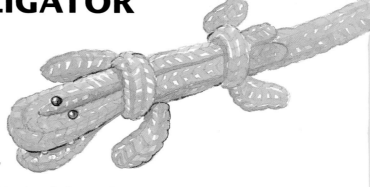

1 Cut one of the pipe cleaners in half. Weave a pipe cleaner into each of the four pieces of small corking the way you did for the Bendable Horse.

2 Bend one long piece of corking in half. Bend the other long piece 8 cm (3 inches) from the end. Place it under the first bent corked piece so the round ends are together.

3 Wrap one short corked piece 5 cm (2 inches) from the rounded end. Wrap the other one 8 cm (3 inches) from the tail end so that it holds all the corked pieces together. Your alligator should now have a head, body, legs and tail.

4 Glue on the eyes. Bend the snout up a little and open the jaws. Glue on eight white beads along the top of the mouth and eight along the bottom for teeth.

Fun ideas to try

♥ Make other bendable corked animals, such as a coiled snake, a lion with a shaggy mane, a giant giraffe or a slowpoke snail.

HAIR SCRUNCHEE

THINGS YOU NEED

about 45 cm (18 inches) of small corking

a length of elastic 25 cm (10 inches) long,
6 mm (¼ inch) wide

medium-sized safety pin

sewing needle, thread

yarn needle

scissors

1 Attach the safety pin to one end of the elastic. Poke it into the end of the corking.

2 Work the elastic down the length of corking, making sure the free end of the elastic stays outside. When you reach the end, poke the elastic through the corking.

3 Overlap the ends of the elastic and use the needle and thread to sew them together.

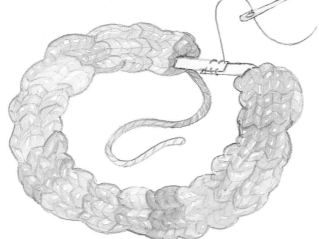

4 Thread the yarn tail on the corking into a yarn needle. Sew the corking ends together to form a circle and cover the elastic.

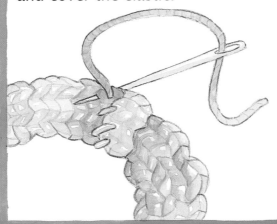

BRAIDED HAIR BAND

THINGS YOU NEED

3 colorful lengths of small corking,
  each about 48 cm (19 inches) long

2 twist ties

yarn needle

scissors

1 Hold the three corked pieces together at one end with a twist tie.

2 Braid them. Use a twist tie to hold the other ends together.

3 Use the yarn needle and the yarn tails to sew together the ends of each piece of corking. Trim the yarn ends.

4 Remove the twist ties and try on your braided hair band or give it as a gift.

Fun ideas to try

Sew a length of corking about 45 cm (18 inches) long into a circle for an easy single hair band.

POT HOLDER

THINGS YOU NEED

2 m (6 ½ feet) of small corking

yarn

yarn needle

scissors

1 Measure and cut an arm's length of yarn. Knot the yarn at one end and thread it into the needle.

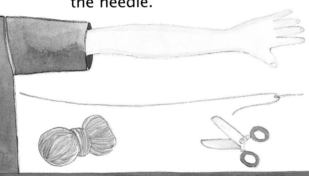

2 Bend the corking into a short, tight "J."

3 Pull the needle and yarn through a couple of stitches from each part of the "J" hook. The stitches should not show on the front of your work. Wind the corking around some more.

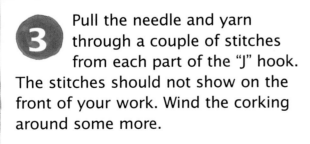

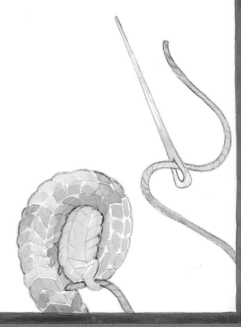

4 Each time you wind more corking around itself, sew it to the corking beside it. Wind and sew the corking loosely, so that it stays flat rather than popping up.

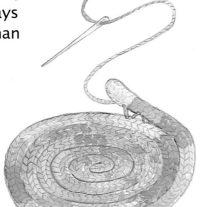

5 When you reach the end of the corking (or run out of yarn) make a couple of stitches in the same spot and weave the yarn into the corking so that it doesn't show. Trim any yarn ends.

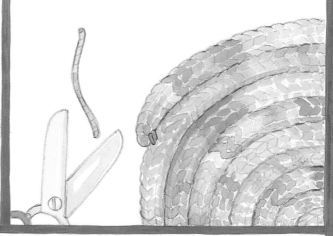

Fun ideas to try

▌▌ Use your pot holder for a doll-house mat or set a plant on it.

▌▌ Make a small pot holder to use as a coaster. You will need about 75 cm (30 inches) of corking.

▌▌ If you would like to make an oval pot holder or place mat, start sewing the corking together in a long, narrow "U" shape. Continue to wind and sew the corking in this oval shape.

▌▌ Corking is a great way to use up leftover yarn. See how many different colors of yarn you can get into your length of corking. By the time you run out of yarn, you may have enough corking to make yourself a bedside mat!

WRITE STUFF

THINGS YOU NEED

strands of small corking

an item of clothing such as a hat, sweater or sweatshirt

chalk or fabric marker

yarn, scissors

a needle with a sharp point and a large hole

1 Draw a simple design or word on the clothing with the chalk or fabric marker.

2 Measure and cut an arm's length of yarn. Knot the yarn at one end and thread it into the needle.

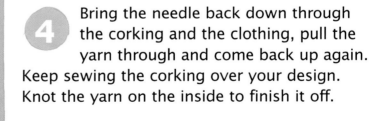

3 Poke the needle through from the inside of the clothing so that the knot doesn't show. Poke through the end of the corking, too.

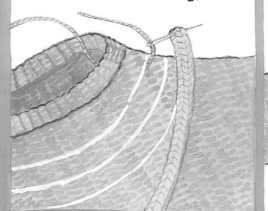

4 Bring the needle back down through the corking and the clothing, pull the yarn through and come back up again. Keep sewing the corking over your design. Knot the yarn on the inside to finish it off.

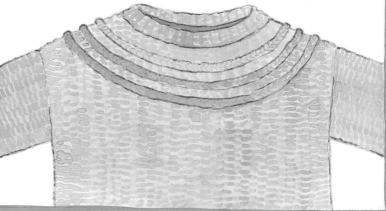

SKINNY CORKING

THINGS YOU NEED
small corker
small ball of yarn

1 Instead of winding the yarn around all four sets of nails, wind it around the two sets of nails across from each other.

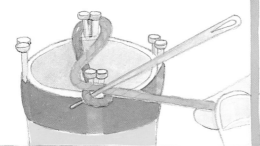

2 You'll be corking on only those two sets of nails. Ignore the other nails. This makes a thin, slightly square-looking cord that grows very quickly.

Fun ideas to try

⭐ Try sewing about 2 m (6 ½ feet) of skinny corking into a circle for a colorful, knot-free string-games string.

⭐ Tie it around a present to add a fun trim.

⭐ Make a bracelet. Tie it on your wrist using the yarn ends.

⭐ In festive colors, skinny corking makes a terrific garland. Tie on bells, baubles and bows for a long-lasting holiday trim.

SLIPPER SOCKS

THINGS YOU NEED

large can corker
2 or 3 different-colored small
   balls of yarn
scissors
yarn needle

1 Cork with one color until you have corked about 15 rows. Count the rows by counting the strands of yarn coming from one set of nails going down into the center of the corker.

2 Cut the yarn, leaving a 5-cm (2-inch) tail. Tie the next color onto it and tuck the knot into the center of the corker.

3 Continue corking and changing colors every 15 rows until you have a tube about 45 cm (18 inches) long. This will make an ankle sock for adults and a slouch sock for kids. Cut the yarn, leaving a 25-cm (10-inch) tail.

4 Thread the tail into the needle. Pick up all the loops of yarn off the nails with the needle so that the loops are now gathered onto the yarn tail.

5 Pull the yarn end tightly. Make a couple of small stitches in the same spot and weave the yarn into the corking so that it does not show. Trim the yarn. Try on your new slipper sock and make another for a matching pair.

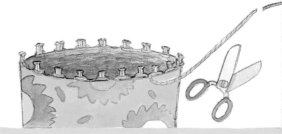

SNAKE DRAFT STOPPER

THINGS YOU NEED

large can corker

2 or 3 different-colored balls
of yarn

scissors

yarn needle

polyester fiberfill stuffing

felt, beads or buttons

sewing needle

thread

1 Cork a colorful tube about 1 m (3 feet) long, closing one end the way you did for the Slipper Socks.

2 Roll the tube down to the closed end. Unroll it as you loosely stuff it with polyester fiberfill to about 15 cm (6 inches) from the end.

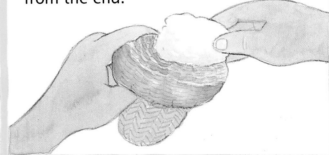

3 Knot the tube to hold in the stuffing.

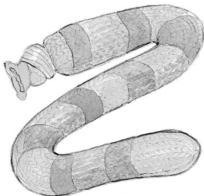

4 Sew on felt, beads or buttons for the eyes. Place it in front of a door to stop the drafts or throw it on your bed for a flexible pillow.

DOLL CLOTHES

THINGS YOU NEED

medium can corker

ball of yarn (multi-colored
  yarn looks nice)

scissors

yarn needle

1 Cork a tube about 20 cm (8 inches) long to make a doll dress. Cut the yarn, leaving a 25-cm (10-inch) tail.

2 Thread the yarn tail into the needle and pick up all the loops of yarn off all the nails.

3 Keep the corked tube open. Make a couple of small stitches in one spot and weave the tail into the corking.

4 Make a skirt and mini-top the same way.

5 If you'd like to make a hat, cork a tube 8 cm (3 inches) long. Pull the yarn tightly as you take it off the corker so that one end is closed. Roll up the edge of the hat and try it on your doll.

BABY MITTENS

THINGS YOU NEED

medium can corker
small ball of yarn
scissors
yarn needle
50 cm (20 inches)
   of satin ribbon

1 Cork a tube about 10 cm (4 inches) long. Cut the yarn, leaving a 25-cm (10-inch) tail.

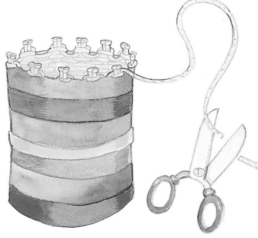

2 Thread the tail into the needle and pick up the loops of yarn off all the nails. Pull the yarn end tightly. Make a couple of small stitches and weave the yarn into the corking. Trim the yarn.

3 Repeat steps 1 and 2 to make another mitten.

4 Cut the piece of ribbon in half. Weave a ribbon around the wrist area of each mitten for decoration and to help them stay on. They make a cosy gift.

CORKED HAMSTER

THINGS YOU NEED

medium can corker
small ball of light-brown yarn
small ball of white yarn
scissors
polyester fiberfill stuffing
yarn needle
small dark buttons or beads

1 Begin corking with the brown yarn. Cork about eight rows. To count the number of rows you have corked, count the strands of yarn coming from one set of nails going down into the center of the corker.

2 Cut the brown yarn, leaving a 5-cm (2-inch) tail, and tie on the white yarn. Tuck the knot into the center of the corker. Cork about eight rows of white and then go back to the brown.

3 When you have completed another eight rows of brown, cut the yarn, leaving a 25-cm (10-inch) tail. Thread the tail into the yarn needle. Use the yarn needle to gather the yarn loops off the corker. Close the end by pulling tightly on the yarn tail. Leave the yarn end on for now.

4 Put some stuffing in the tube. Sew the other end closed with the needle and brown yarn. Leave a short tail of yarn as you finish. This is the hamster's tail.

5 Use the piece of yarn at the hamster's head to sew on button or bead eyes. Make a couple of small stitches in the same spot as you finish sewing on the eyes to secure them. Trim the yarn.

6 Cut a 20-cm (8-inch) piece of brown yarn and thread it into the needle. Bring the yarn through the top of the hamster's head. Remove the needle and tie the yarn into a bow to make the ears. Double knot the bow and trim the yarn ends.

7 For whiskers, cut two or three 10-cm (4-inch) pieces of white yarn and thread them one at a time through the hamster's nose. Tie them in a knot.

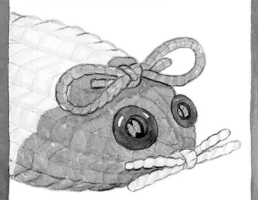

Fun ideas to try

☺ Make other stuffed creatures by following the same steps but changing the features. For example, make a mouse out of gray yarn and leave a long yarn tail. Or make a rabbit with a little pom-pom tail.

☺ Try using small corking to make legs for your creatures. For example, make a green frog body with the medium can corker and use the small corker to make four green legs. Stuff the body and sew on the legs. Add big eyes (buttons, yarn or mini-pom-poms) and you're finished. Ribbet!

FINGER PUPPETS

THINGS YOU NEED

small can corker

small ball of yarn

scissors

yarn needle

yarn, buttons, felt, moving eyes,
  pipe cleaners and beads

sewing needle and thread
  or white glue

1 Cork a tube about 8 cm (3 inches) long. Use the yarn tail and needle to close one end of the tube.

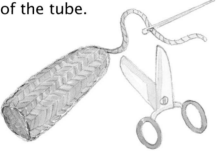

2 Sew or glue on a face. Make hair with felt or yarn.

3 Make a few, and not only will you have fun with different characters, you'll also keep your fingers warm!

HAND PUPPETS

THINGS YOU NEED

corked tube from a large can corker,
   30 cm (12 inches) long, closed at one end

scissors

yarn needle

pencil, fabric marker or chalk pencil

yarn, buttons, felt, moving eyes, pipe
   cleaners and beads

sewing needle and thread or white glue

1 Put your hand inside the corked tube and push the closed end of the tube in between your thumb and fingers. Mark where you would like to make the eyes and nose.

2 For the eyes, glue or sew on buttons, beads or moving eyes. Use a pom-pom, felt or a button to make a nose.

3 From the felt, cut out long and floppy, short and pointy, small and round or any other shaped ears. Sew or glue them in place.

4 For finishing touches, try a long piece of small corking for an elephant's trunk, pipe cleaner whiskers for a cat, or many different-colored pieces of yarn for a horse or lion mane. What will you need to make a dragon or space creature?

SCARF AND HEADBAND

THINGS YOU NEED

huge can corker
large ball of yarn
scissors
yarn needle

1 You will likely find the huge corker easiest to hold on your lap or between your knees. Wind the yarn around the nails as you did for the other corkers, but when you reach the last set of nails, stop. Make a complete circle around this last set of nails and wind the yarn back the way you just came. There should be two lines of yarn on the last and second-last sets of nails.

2 Don't cork the last set of nails. Cork the second-last set and continue back in that direction until you reach the first set of nails with the slip knot on them.

3 Cork the first set of nails and, once again, start winding the yarn back the way you came. Cork the first set again and continue on to the second and so on.

4 When you reach the last set of nails this time, lift both lower strands of yarn over the new top one, bring the yarn back around and cork this set of nails again. Cork back the way you came.

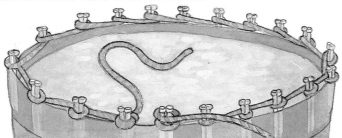

5 Keep corking back and forth between the last and first sets of nails so that you never complete the circle. Cork very loosely. Remember to loosen the stitch you have just corked as you go.

6 Cork until your scarf is about 120 cm (48 inches) long. Cut the yarn, leaving a 60-cm (24-inch) tail. Thread the yarn tail into the needle and gather the loops of yarn off all the nails. Stretch out this edge, knot the yarn tail and weave it into the scarf.

7 Your scarf will roll in at the edges but you can easily unroll it to put it around your head or up over your chin. It will also feel very soft and warm wound loosely around your neck. Always tuck the ends inside your coat.

8 To make a matching headband, make a length of corking about 45 cm (18 inches) long using the huge corker. This time, cork in the usual circular way. Instead of pulling tightly on the yarn when you take your work off the corker, keep it wide. Cut a long tail and use it to sew the ends of the band together to make a circle. (You can also make a headband using your large can corker.)

Fun ideas to try

● Make a fringe on your scarf. Wind two or three different colors of yarn around a 15 cm x 10 cm (6 inch x 4 inch) cardboard rectangle about 80 times. Cut only one end of the yarn. Take about three cut pieces of yarn at a time and hold them folded in half. Pull open two or three stitches along one short end of the scarf. Push the loop end of the fringe pieces into the stitches. Open the loop and bring through the ends. Pull tight. Continue until both ends are fringed. Trim the fringe if you like.

MAKING POM-POMS

THINGS YOU NEED
ball of yarn
scissors

1 Cut a piece of yarn about one arm's length. Cut it in half. Set this yarn aside.

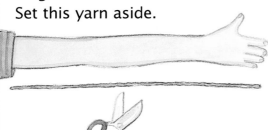

2 Hold your index and middle fingers of one hand slightly apart as you very loosely start winding yarn from your ball around them.

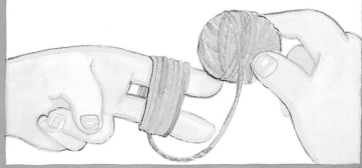

3 Depending on the size of your fingers and the thickness of the yarn, you will need to wind the yarn between 50 and 100 times. Wind it loosely enough so that it doesn't hurt, and keep a space between your fingers. Cut the yarn from the ball.

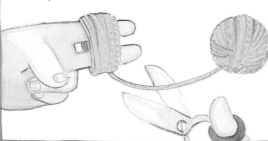

4 Take the pieces of yarn you cut and push them in between your fingers on each side of the wound yarn. Tie them loosely with a double loop as shown. Very gently slide the yarn off your fingers.

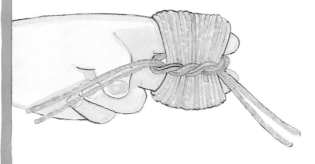

5 Tie the yarn as tightly as you can in the center of the bundle of yarn. Triple knot the tying yarn as shown here.

6 Cut open all the loops and trim your pom-pom. Hit it against the edge of a table to fluff it and see if it needs any more trimming. The more you trim your pom-pom, the smaller and thicker it will get. Don't trim off the tying yarn ends — you may need them to tie your pom-pom onto other projects.

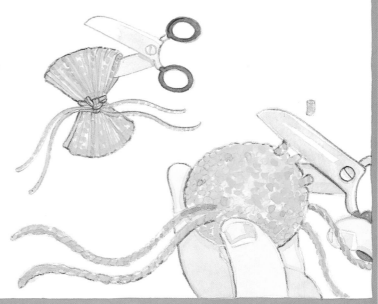

Fun ideas to try

✿ Experiment with many types and thicknesses of yarn.

✿ Wind on more than one color of yarn for a multi-colored pom-pom.

✿ If you want a large pom-pom, wind the yarn around three or four of your fingers. Be sure to tie the pom-pom in the center.

POM-POMS ON CORKING

Golf Club Cover Cork a tube about 20 cm (8 inches) long on a large can corker and finish it off as you would a sock. Tie a pom-pom on the top and that's all there is to it! Make a set of three as a gift.

Pom-pom Fringe Make a whole bunch of different-colored mini-pom-poms. Use the yarn ends to tie them onto your corked scarf for a pom-pom fringe.

Bookmark Tie a small pom-pom onto a 30-cm (12-inch) length of skinny corking and tuck it between the pages of your book.

Ponytail Holder If you sew a pom-pom on each end of a length of corking, it makes a wonderful hair band or ponytail holder. It also looks nice just hanging on your bedroom doorknob.

Gift Tie Cork an extra-long piece of skinny corking. Tie or sew a pom-pom onto each end. Tie it around a newspaper-wrapped gift to add pizzazz!

Other Fun Ideas Tie a couple of pom-poms on your headband, slipper socks, baby mittens or puppets.